This Gift Log Book

belongs to:

....

Gift log

gift received	given by	thank you sent

Notes:

Gift log

gift received	given by	thank you sent

Notes:

Gift log

gift received	given by	thank you sent

Notes:

Gift log

gift received	given by	thank you sent

Notes:

Gift log

gift received	given by	thank you sent

Notes:

Gift log

gift received	given by	thank you sent

Notes:

Gift log

gift received	given by	thank you sent

Notes:

Gift log

gift received	given by	thank you sent

Notes:

Gift log

gift received	given by	thank you sent

Notes:

Gift log

gift received	given by	thank you sent

Notes:

Gift log

gift received	given by	thank you sent

Notes:

Gift log

gift received	given by	thank you sent

Notes:

Gift log

gift received	given by	thank you sent

Notes:

Gift log

gift received	given by	thank you sent

Notes:

Gift log

gift received	given by	thank you sent

Notes:

Gift log

gift received	given by	thank you sent

Notes:

Gift log

gift received	given by	thank you sent

Notes:

Gift log

gift received	given by	thank you sent

Notes:

Gift log

gift received	given by	thank you sent

Notes:

Gift log

gift received	given by	thank you sent

Notes:

Gift log

gift received	given by	thank you sent

Notes:

Gift log

gift received	given by	thank you sent

Notes:

Gift log

gift received	given by	thank you sent

Notes:

Gift log

gift received	given by	thank you sent

Notes:

Gift log

gift received	given by	thank you sent

Notes:

Gift log

gift received	given by	thank you sent

Notes:

Gift log

gift received	given by	thank you sent

Notes:

Gift log

gift received	given by	thank you sent

Notes:

Gift log

gift received	given by	thank you sent

Notes:

Gift log

gift received	given by	thank you sent

Notes:

Gift log

gift received	given by	thank you sent

Notes:

Gift log

gift received	given by	thank you sent

Notes:

Gift log

gift received	given by	thank you sent

Notes:

Gift log

gift received	given by	thank you sent

Notes:

Gift log

gift received	given by	thank you sent

Notes:

Gift log

gift received	given by	thank you sent

Notes:

Gift log

gift received	given by	thank you sent

Notes:

Gift log

gift received	given by	thank you sent

Notes:

Gift log

gift received	given by	thank you sent

Notes:

Gift log

gift received	given by	thank you sent

Notes:

Gift log

gift received	given by	thank you sent

Notes:

Gift log

gift received	given by	thank you sent

Notes:

Gift log

gift received	given by	thank you sent

Notes:

Gift log

gift received	given by	thank you sent

Notes:

Gift log

gift received	given by	thank you sent

Notes:

Gift log

gift received	given by	thank you sent

Notes:

Gift log

gift received	given by	thank you sent

Notes:

Gift log

gift received	given by	thank you sent

Notes:

Gift log

gift received	given by	thank you sent

Notes:

Gift log

gift received	given by	thank you sent

Notes:

Gift log

gift received	given by	thank you sent

Notes:

Gift log

gift received	given by	thank you sent

Notes:

Gift log

gift received	given by	thank you sent

Notes:

Gift log

gift received	given by	thank you sent

Notes:

Gift log

gift received	given by	thank you sent

Notes:

Gift log

gift received	given by	thank you sent

Notes:

Gift log

gift received	given by	thank you sent

Notes:

Gift log

gift received	given by	thank you sent

Notes:

Gift log

gift received	given by	thank you sent

Notes:

Gift log

gift received	given by	thank you sent

Notes:

Gift log

gift received	given by	thank you sent

Notes:

Gift log

gift received	given by	thank you sent

Notes:

Gift log

gift received	given by	thank you sent

Notes:

Gift log

gift received	given by	thank you sent

Notes:

Gift log

gift received	given by	thank you sent

Notes:

Gift log

gift received	given by	thank you sent

Notes:

Gift log

gift received	given by	thank you sent

Notes:

Gift log

gift received	given by	thank you sent

Notes:

Gift log

gift received	given by	thank you sent

Notes:

Gift log

gift received	given by	thank you sent

Notes:

Gift log

gift received	given by	thank you sent

Notes:

Gift log

gift received	given by	thank you sent

Notes:

Gift log

gift received	given by	thank you sent

Notes:

Gift log

gift received	given by	thank you sent

Notes:

Gift log

gift received	given by	thank you sent

Notes:

Gift log

gift received	given by	thank you sent

Notes:

Gift log

gift received	given by	thank you sent

Notes:

Gift log

gift received	given by	thank you sent

Notes:

Gift log

gift received	given by	thank you sent

Notes:

Gift log

gift received	given by	thank you sent

Notes:

Gift log

gift received	given by	thank you sent

Notes:

Gift log

gift received	given by	thank you sent

Notes:

Gift log

gift received	given by	thank you sent

Notes:

Gift log

gift received	given by	thank you sent

Notes:

Gift log

gift received	given by	thank you sent

Notes:

Gift log

gift received	given by	thank you sent

Notes:

Gift log

gift received	given by	thank you sent

Notes:

Gift log

gift received	given by	thank you sent

Notes:

Gift log

gift received	given by	thank you sent

Notes:

Gift log

gift received	given by	thank you sent

Notes:

Gift log

gift received	given by	thank you sent

Notes:

Gift log

gift received	given by	thank you sent

Notes:

Gift log

gift received	given by	thank you sent

Notes:

Gift log

gift received	given by	thank you sent

Notes:

Gift log

gift received	given by	thank you sent

Notes:

Gift log

gift received	given by	thank you sent

Notes:

Gift log

gift received	given by	thank you sent

Notes:

Gift log

gift received	given by	thank you sent

Notes:

Gift log

gift received	given by	thank you sent

Notes:

Gift log

gift received	given by	thank you sent

Notes:

Gift log

gift received	given by	thank you sent

Notes:

Gift log

gift received	given by	thank you sent

Notes:

Gift log

gift received	given by	thank you sent

Notes:

Gift log

gift received	given by	thank you sent

Notes:

Gift log

gift received	given by	thank you sent

Notes:

Gift log

gift received	given by	thank you sent

Notes:

Gift log

gift recieved	given by	thank you sent

Notes:

Impressum

Jan-Pascal Dejon
Gebbertstraße 12
91052 Erlangen
dejon.jan@gmail.com

Made in United States
Orlando, FL
02 June 2022

18427772R00063